Addison's Disease in Dogs

Addison's Disease in Dogs. Copyright © 2009 by Stephanie Kenrose. All rights reserved.

Cover art: Peet@Flickr.com

ISBN 1449513077

For Shakti-Holly, my shadow and best friend.

Contents

CONTENTS 5

CHAPTER ONE: INTRODUCTION 7

CHAPTER TWO: WHAT IS ADDISON'S DISEASE? 13

CHAPTER THREE: SYMPTOMS 19

CHAPTER FOUR: CAUSES 23

   Do Vaccinations Cause Addison's disease? 25

   Titer Testing—an alternative to vaccines 29

CHAPTER FIVE: DIAGNOSIS 33

   ACTH test 35

CHAPTER SIX: GENETICS AND INHERITABILITY 37

   How inheritability works 39

CHAPTER SEVEN: TREATMENT OPTIONS 45

   Treatment for Primary Addison's Disease 47

   Side effects of medication 48

   Percorten-V side effects: 48

   Prednisone Side Effects and Florinef (fludrocortisone acetate) Side Effects 49

   Treatment for Secondary Addison's Disease 50

   What happens if my dog doesn't receive prednisone? 51

CHAPTER: CHEAPER TREATMENT OPTIONS 53

   Long Term Stress Management 58

APPENDIX 1 NOTE ON HEARTWORM PREVENTATIVE MEDICINES 59

DEFINITIONS 63

REFERENCES 69

ACKNOWLEDGMENTS 75

INDEX 77

Chapter One: Introduction

We welcomed our wonderful border collie, Shakti-Holly into our family in January 2007. She was very young–about a year old–and had been left for dead at a veterinarian by her previous owners. One day, a year and a half after she came to live with us, Shakti-Holly started acting lethargic. She didn't want to go for her usual walk, and she didn't want to eat—not even a treat. Less than twenty four hours later, she was in shock, with multiple organs failing.

We adopted Shakti-Holly from a Border collie rescue facility about an hour's drive south from our home in Northern Florida. Holly (as she was called then) was very young—the rescue estimated that she was about a year old. A few months before coming to the rescue, Holly found herself at the local dog pound. A man and woman adopted her, but soon after arriving home Holly became severely ill. Her owner's took her to a veterinarian, who suspected Holly had been poisoned: her liver was shutting down, he told the new owners, and it was probably going to cost several hundred dollars to treat her—that's if she survived at all.

"Go ahead and put her to sleep," they said. "We can get another one at the pound for sixty bucks."

Instead of euthanizing Holly, the vet started her on IV fluids and nursed her back to health. After only a few days, Holly was back to good health, fully recovered from the mysterious "poisoning." The vet called a local Border collie rescue, who took her in.

A few weeks later, my husband, two sons and I visited the rescue looking for a new addition to our family.

"I have just the girl for you!" the rescue's owner, Jerry said, when we met her at her kennels.

I think we all imagined taking home an energetic, agile herding dog—like the border collies I'd seen at sheepdog trials, mercilessly forcing 50 sheep into a pen.

The pathetic bundle of bones that slinked toward us with ears and tail tightly held down in a submissive pose wasn't quite what I'd had in mind. Holly's coat was thin, her tail as spindly as a piece of old rope. Her thin coat, Jerry told us, was due to the previous liver failure. "Don't worry," she said. "It'll grow back."[1]

Holly looked like she wouldn't say boo to a goose, let alone bark at strangers or play tag with a loud, rambunctious eight-year-old. Despite Jerry's reassurances that there was a real dog under the sheep's clothing, we weren't sure.

We looked at several other dogs, all of whom looked so sweet and needful of a home that we had a hard time deciding. However, Holly kept tugging at our heart strings, so after spending about two hours trying to make up our minds, we decided that Jerry—with her decades of experience with border collies—probably knew what she was talking about.

We took Holly home in January, 2007, renaming her Shakti after the Hindu goddess (following a tradition in our family to name our pets after gods and goddesses). We started to call her Shakti-Holly so that she would get used to her new name,

---

[1] I should probably note that we don't blame the rescue in any way for not knowing that Holly had Addison's disease. The veterinarian had given her a clean bill of health. It wasn't the vet's fault either—Addison's is notoriously difficult to diagnose.

but the full name stuck for many months (even years later, we still occasionally call her Shakti-Holly, especially when she's "herding" the mailman and refuses to come in). It took several months of back rubs, daily trips to the park and cuddles on the couch to build up her confidence but she was soon "protecting" her herd (us) from the UPS guy, passing wheelchairs and small children.

Shakti's tail and coat grew long and fluffy and people would stop us out on walks to comment on what a beautiful dog she was. Her tail would constantly wag—going to the park, coming home from the park, getting a treat, receiving a scratch, waking up in the morning, or even going to sleep. I would joke that all I had to do to clean the kitchen floor was to bring Shakti into the kitchen and get her to sit on the floor: her swishing tail would do the rest.

Then one day in September 2008, Shakti's tail stopped wagging.

I couldn't put my finger on what was wrong, but she was acting strangely depressed, vomiting and refusing to eat. My veterinarian thought it was probably viral and took some blood just to make sure, instructing me to call back in 48 hours for the lab results. However, the following day, Shakti's health deteriorated rapidly. By the afternoon she was starting to wobble and looked ready to keel over.

I scooped her into the car and drove to an emergency vet. An hour later, the vet informed us that the in-house lab results indicated Addison's disease, and that he wanted to do an ACTH (adrenocorticotropic hormone stimulation) test which was the only way to confirm the presence of Addison's disease.

Apparently, JFK had Addison's and hid it well, but it wasn't a disease I was familiar with. "Addison's? What's that?" I asked.

The vet told me that Addison's is a disease where the adrenal glands stop producing the hormones that regulate, amongst a whole host of other things, electrolytes in the blood. Shakti was experiencing bradycardia (a slow heart rate), and if she didn't receive emergency medical care immediately, the high potassium levels and low sodium in the blood would cause her heart to stop.

I agreed to the ACTH test and Shakti's front leg was shaved for administration of IV fluids. When I left her at the vets for six hours (we weren't allowed back in the room where they were giving fluids) my heart panged and I hoped that she didn't think she was being dumped again. In retrospect I think she was in such bad shape that she probably didn't care much about anything.

The ACTH test confirmed the diagnosis of Addison's disease. The fix was relatively easy: fluids, hormones, and a brief afternoon rest at the vets. Shakti left the veterinarians office wagging her tail with a standing prescription for replacement hormones, which she receives once a month.

Shakti has been in relatively good health since that time, although we have to follow a few guidelines: we keep a close eye on her mood and adjust the medication if necessary, she can't be allowed to get stressed, and of course, she's at the vet for a quick checkup every month–and will be for the rest of her life.

Chapter Two: What is Addison's Disease?

In 1849, Thomas Addison wrote about a then-untreatable adrenal gland dysfunction. A century later, in 1953, the first case of Addison's in dogs was recorded.[2] Also known as hypoadrenocorticism, adrenal insufficiency, or hypocortisolism, Addison's disease occurs when the adrenal glands fail to produce enough hormones to keep the body functioning normally. This includes the hormone cortisol.

While cortisol is physically released from the adrenal glands (located above the kidneys—see diagram on the next page), cortisol production is actually controlled by *the pituitary*

---

[2] See Plotnick, 2001.

gland at the base of the brain. The pituitary gland produces adrenocorticotropic hormone (ACTH) which signals the adrenal glands to produce cortisol. A second hormone produced by the adrenal cortex is aldosterone, which together with cortisol assists in regulating dozens of bodily functions, including:

- blood pressure
- cardiovascular function
- immune system inflammatory response
- insulin balance
- metabolism of proteins, carbohydrates, and fats

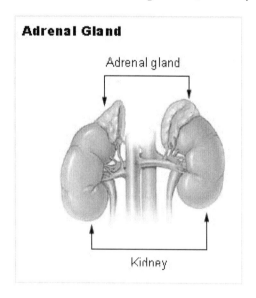

Adrenal Gland

There are two types of Addison's disease:

Primary Addison's disease is when a problem exists with the adrenal gland itself. All dogs with primary Addison's will develop electrolyte imbalances (although it may show up months or even years after the initial diagnosis). Just because a dog has normal electrolytes doesn't mean that it doesn't have Addison's disease--this is one reason why it can be a difficult disease to diagnose. When Shakti had her first crash her electrolytes may have been normal and so her vet would not have suspected Addison's. However, during her second Addisonian crisis, her electrolyte levels went haywire.

A second issue confounding a diagnosis is that primary Addison's is further subdivided into typical and atypical Addison's. *Typical* Addison's means that the adrenal glands are not working and not producing both cortisol and aldosterone (this could be because of disease, hereditary factors, or many other reasons--see Chapter four: Causes). *Atypical* Addison's is where only a *part* of the adrenal cortex isn't working—the part that makes cortisol. Dogs with atypical Addison's will appear to have normal sodium and potassium levels, making a diagnosis even more difficult.[3]

---

[3] To some veterinarians, "atypical" doesn't necessarily mean that the dog is deficient in cortisol—it could mean that they don't have the classic electrolyte changes (i.e. low sodium and high potassium) seen in primary Addison's. See references: Novartis roundtable.

Secondary Addison's disease means that the pituitary gland has stopped working properly. Secondary Addison's disease does not cause electrolyte imbalances, because aldosterone is still produced by the adrenal cortex.

Your veterinarian will be able to differentiate primary from secondary Addison's disease by looking at ACTH or aldosterone levels in the body. With primary Addison's disease, concentrations of ACTH will be high because the pituitary glands

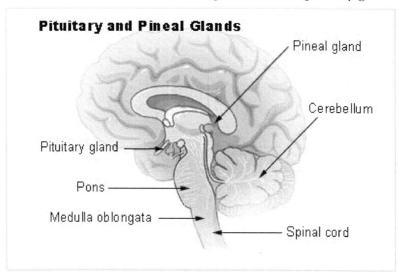

Pituitary and Pineal Glands

are working normally: with secondary Addison's disease, levels will be very low. Secondary Addison's disease is less expensive to treat, but is much rarer than primary Addison's.

Addison's disease occurs much more frequently in dogs than in humans—according to veterinarian Bob McCaskill, it's thought to occur one hundred times more often in the canine population than in people. This is most likely because of the inbreeding that happens in dog populations—inherited diseases are more likely to crop up if only a select number of dogs are used for breeding, as is the case with pedigreed dogs.

Addison's disease mainly affects young to middle-age female dogs like Shakti-Holly, who was about 20 months old at diagnosis. The average age at diagnosis is four years (although it has been found in puppies and dogs up to 12 years old). The majority of afflicted dogs (about two thirds) are female. Certain breeds are more susceptible to the disease than other: great Danes, Portuguese water dogs, standard poodles, West Highland white terriers, bearded collies, rottweilers, Springer spaniels, German Shorthaired Pointers, Soft-Coated Wheaten Terriers, and Nova Scotia duck tolling retrievers have all higher than normal rates of Addison's disease than other breeds. Several breeds are particularly *not* susceptible to Addison's: American pit bull terriers, American Staffordshire terriers, Chihuahuas, cocker spaniels, golden retrievers, Lhasa Apsos, schnauzers, and Yorkshire Terriers are all less likely to have Addison's disease. However, whatever breed of dog you own, you should be aware of the symptoms of Addison's disease—it could strike any dog, at any time and without prompt medical attention your pet could be dead within hours if not treated with emergency medical care.

Chapter Three: Symptoms

Symptoms of Addison's disease can be so nonspecific that they are commonly attributed to other diseases. That's why it's so important to take your dog to the vet when they are ill–something as simple as an upset stomach could be something much more serious.

Dogs with Addison's disease might at first appear to have a gastrointestinal disease–they might be vomiting, have diarrhea and a poor appetite. You might also notice that they drink more frequently and urinate more often. The signs may be so subtle that you don't notice any signs at all–that is until they have an Addisonian crisis and collapse. A dog can go from being fine to having an Addisonian crisis in just a few hours.

An Addisonian crisis is a medical emergency. Symptoms can be vague and mimic gastrointestinal disorders (diarrhea), acute renal failure (kidney failure), liver disease, insulinoma (too much insulin), hypothyroidism (underactive thyroid) or hypoglycemia (low blood sugar). Here are the symptoms that are generally indicative of an Addisonian crisis:

- lethargy
- slow heart rate (bradycardia)
- not eating
- drinking and urinating frequently
- severe weakness
- vomiting blood (rare)
- blood in the stool (rare)
- black, tarry stool (rare)
- seizures due to hypoglycemia (rare)

The vast majority of dogs with Addison's disease who go to a veterinarian for treatment will be in serious condition, with severe symptoms like lethargy, depression, and poor or no appetite. Your dog will also likely be vomiting, weak, and might have lost weight. Many dogs will be dehydrated and have diarrhea. Some might have collapsed, have a weak pulse or a slow heart rate (bradycardia), or show a slow capillary refill time (to measure capillary refill time, press a thumb firmly on your dogs gum for about five seconds. Release the thumb and count: the amount of time it takes the gum to return to normal should be about one second). One diagnostic clue is if your dog has a history of illness in the past where they get ill when stressed and get better with rest or a simple therapy like IV fluids. We found one such clue with Shakti's past—when her previous owners left her for dead at the veterinarians. She responded well to IV therapy at the veterinarians and made a 100% recovery from what was presumed to be a poisoning or liver failure. Looking back, this could have been the first sign of Addison's, and I can only guess at what stressed her out before she was dumped.

Your dog may only have some of the above symptoms—or they may have different symptoms. Unfortunately, these signs can also indicate a host of other disorders. Addison's symptoms can be easily mistaken for a gastrointestinal disorder or even anorexia (a refusal to eat). At first, it might seem that your dog has acute renal failure, liver disease, insulinoma, or hypothyroidism.

When I took Shakti, to my original vet with weakness and a refusal to eat, the vet thought she had a virus. Two days later, Shakti went into a full-blown Addisonian crisis and nearly died. A small practice veterinarian might only see one or two cases of Canine Addison's in a year and a hundred cases of gastrointestinal viruses so unfortunately it can be easy to miss a diagnosis of Addison's.

Is it any wonder that Addison's disease has been called "The Great Pretender"?

Chapter Four: Causes

As of time of writing (2009), the causes of Addison's disease aren't exactly known but there are several suspects, including a faulty immune system, vaccinations, and tumors:

- *Faulty Immune System.* Many veterinarians believe that most cases of primary Addison's disease occur because the immune system attacks the adrenal glands and destroys them. The reasons for this are mostly unknown. However, the inherited immune disorder granulomatous disease (a disorder in which immune cells called phagocytes don't work properly) can be a cause of Addison's.

- *Genetics:* According to Drs. Chase et. al— researchers at the university of Ohio's department of biology— Addison's occurs between 1.5% and 9% of domestic dogs, depending on the breed. Bearded collies have a particularly high susceptibility to canine Addison's. The Canine Genetic Analysis Project (CGAP) at the University of California found that out of 1470 Bearded Collies tested in the program (as of 2005), 92 had Addison's disease, suggestive of a high heritability and the possibility of a single recessive gene responsible for Addison's disease. The team is still gathering data (as of 2009) for many breeds. More information on CGAP is available in the Web Resources section of this book.

- *Cancer:* Cancer of the pituitary gland, adrenal lymphoma, or cancer that has spread to the adrenal glands from somewhere else (i.e. the lung or non-Hodgkin's lymphoma) can cause Addison's disease.

- *Drugs:* Addison's disease can occur because of drugs that block corticosteroid synthesis in the body. For example, the *Veterinary Drug Handbook* lists Ketoconazole–used in dogs and cats to treat fungal infections—as possibly causing symptoms of Addison's disease. An overdose of mitotane (a drug used to treat cancer of the adrenal glands) can also cause Addison's disease.

- *Inflammation/trauma*: any kind of damage to the adrenal gland can cause Addison's disease. It could be from something as simple as an infection or something as major as a car accident.

Most items in the above list could pertain to primary or secondary Addison's disease. Secondary Addison's disease is caused by pituitary gland problems, and like primary Addison's can be caused by many different factors including inflammation, trauma, genetics, and tumors.

Do Vaccinations Cause Addison's disease?

Some schools of thought have suggested vaccinations may trigger immune system disorders.[4] Most of us visit the veterinarian once a year with Fluffy or Rover for yearly vaccinations, thinking that we are responsible pet owners for remembering that yearly visit. I never gave this annual event a second thought until Shakti developed her Addison's disease and I conducted some research into the possible causes. I discovered that vaccines are thought in some circles to cause immune disorders in dogs, so I'll be foregoing her usual annual shots in favor of titer tests.

---

[4] See Duval and Giger's 1996 study where 15 of 58 dogs at the Veterinary Hospital of the University of Pennsylvania over a 27 month period developed idiopathic IMHA (immune-mediated hemolytic anaemia) within one month after vaccinations.

Shortly after Shakti was diagnosed with Addisons, a post on an Addison's discussion forum caught my eye: a woman who said her poodle, "Timmy", came down with Addison's disease two and a half weeks after he received his annual booster shots. This came at the time when Shakti was due for her annual booster—four months after her initial Addison's diagnosis. I decided to look into vaccinations before I took Shakti for her yearly check up. I was shocked to learn that these annual visits aren't actually recommended by any major organization or drug manufacturer and may actually be harming our dogs.[5]

Most dogs are vaccinated annually against distemper, leptospirosis, canine adenovirus-1 & hepatitis, canine parainfluenza virus, canine parvovirus, canine Corona virus as well as canine bordatella (kennel cough) and Lyme disease. Vaccines work by stimulating the immune system to produce antibodies to a particular disease; if the dog is exposed at a later date to the pathogen, antibodies will attack and neutralize the disease.

The "puppy shots" (those vaccinations given in puppyhood), are recommended by most veterinarians. It's the adult booster shots that are causing the most controversy. Until recently, vaccine manufacturers recommended that all dogs be

---

[5] I have excluded rabies from this discussion: most states require regular rabies shots once a year—consult your local animal control department for details.

given a booster shot once a year. Veterinarians were in agreement—yearly booster shots are a way to encourage animal owners to visit every year and increase income. However, in 2003, the American Animal Hospital Association (AAHA) released new guidelines and recommendations for shots that differed from the once a year visit that most pet owners were used to.

The AAHA designated four core vaccines that are necessary because of the serious nature of the pathogens: distemper, parvovirus, adenovirus-2, and rabies. For distemper, parvovirus, and adenovirus-2, the recommendations are:

- Vaccinate at 6-8 weeks, 9-11 weeks, and 12-14 weeks.

- Give a booster shot at one year old.

- Subsequent booster shots should be administered every three years unless indicated otherwise (i.e. dogs at high risk may need more frequent shots and owners of dogs with immune disorders may want to forego shots for their pets in favor of titer tests).

There are many factors that an owner needs to take into consideration when deciding how often to vaccinate (and which diseases to vaccinate against), including:

- Reported duration of immunity from each shot (not all drugs are created equal; shots from different manufacturers will have different durations).

- Health and lifestyle of each pet (i.e. indoor vs. outdoor).

- Probability of contracting any particular disease (i.e. working dogs are exposed to more infectious agents than family pets). Dogs that roam, who have contact with wild animals or swim in streams are all at higher risk from contracting disease.

- Public health concerns (i.e. rabies shots are required frequently by law).

Pfizer, one of the major manufacturers of dog vaccines, reported in a study published in the Journal of American Veterinary Medicine in January 2004 that vaccines can protect a dog for four years or more, giving credence to the new guidelines issues by the AAHA. Other studies have found that immunity can last up to seven years.

As Shakti definitely falls into the category of "immune-compromised," I chose to forego her annual shots from now on. Additionally, she's at low risk for most diseases: she stays at home when we are away (we have a pet sitter), and she rarely plays with other dogs—even at the dog park, she keeps to herself. Every couple of years I'll get a titer test done to make sure she is fully immunized against the major diseases.

When the time comes to revaccinate (which I hope we can put off for many years, perhaps even a lifetime), I'll weigh the risk of possible side effects with the risk of her contracting a life-threatening illness. If she does need a shot, I'll ask my vet to get a vaccine from a company that does not put additives into their shots: Intervet is one such company, another is Heska, which produces intranasal vaccines.

Titer Testing—an alternative to vaccines

Titer tests measure how much antibody to a certain pathogen is in your dog's system at the time of the test. Several titer tests are available on the market: your veterinarian may have them or you may need to ask your vet to special order them. Titer tests are available for major diseases like distemper and parvovirus. There's also a rabies titer test available but this does not substitute for proof of rabies protection—you must still comply with local laws and have your dog vaccinated even if they have a positive titer test. Research has shown that up to 95.1% of dogs were protected against parvovirus one to two years after their last vaccinations.[6] However, titer tests are not a perfect

---

[6] See Twark and Dodds, 2000.

alternative and come with their own set of issues including false negatives.[7]

After your pet's blood is drawn, the lab will dilute the blood sample. If the blood is diluted 1,000 times and antibodies are still present, your pet's ratio would show up as 1:1000 on the test form. For parvovirus, a protective titer should be above 1:80 and for distemper, above 1:96 is considered protective. If your dog has a value higher than these figures, it means that your dog does not need a booster shot. The lab will record your pet's titer as "low" or "high" along with the ratio.

At first, a titer test seems like a good alternative to re-vaccinating: if your dog's titer shows high antibodies—great! If antibodies are low, then it would seem a good time to vaccinate. However, titer tests don't work quite that simply, and a low titer could cause you to give an unnecessary booster shot.

A 2002 report from the American Veterinary Medical Association did state that titer testing is, for the most part, unreliable. However, many others advocate titer tests as a guide to determine whether you should vaccinate your pet. If you are

---

[7] Researchers Morre & Glickman (2004) state that in a hypothetical group of 1,000 dogs tested, 86 might have false negative titers. Still, 86 dogs vaccinated unnecessarily might be better than all 1,000 being revaccinated, which is what would happen without the availability of a titer test.

considering a titer blood test in lieu of vaccinating, the ultimate decision is up to you–but in an immune compromised dog with Addison's disease, a titer test just might be the right choice.

Chapter Five: Diagnosis

A simple blood test may alert your veterinarian to the possibility of your dog having Addison's disease. The classic signs for Addison's are:

- hyperkalemia: elevated potassium level due to lack of the adrenal hormone aldosterone.
- hyponatremia : low sodium level, also due to lack of aldosterone.
- azotemia: elevated kidney parameters, i.e. high urea in the blood as shown by the serum BUN (blood urea nitrogen) level test.
- hypochloremia: low levels of chloride in the blood.

- metabolic acidosis: low bicarbonate levels, causing blood that is too acidic.
- absence of a stress leukogram. Sick dogs normally release cortisol, causing a characteristic white blood cell pattern. Addison's dogs cannot mount a stress response due to the lack of cortisol coming from the adrenal cortex; thus, their white blood cell picture will appear to be normal despite their sick appearance.
- There may also be low cholesterol levels in the blood (hypocholesterolemia) or low protein levels (hypoproteinemia) and abnormal liver enzyme changes.

These are the classic signs but sometimes they might be absent. For example, just because the sodium level is normal doesn't mean that your dog does not have Addison's disease: it could mean that your Addison's dog is dehydrated (Addison's disease would cause the sodium to go down, but dehydration would cause the level to go up and appear normal). If your dog has vomiting or diarrhea, your veterinarian will want to give your dog fluids to rehydrate them before looking at sodium and potassium levels, which look significantly different in a normally hydrated animal. To confound the issue even further, high potassium and low sodium levels can also be found with other disorders (i.e. whipworms). Whipworm (trichuriasis) has been called "pseudo Addison's" because it closely matches the symptomology. That's why it's vital an adrenocorticotropic hormone stimulation (ACTH) test is performed to confirm a suspected diagnosis. A normally working pituitary gland releases adrenocorticotropic hormone (ACTH) to signal the adrenal glands to produce cortisol. An ACTH stimulation test stimulates the pituitary gland into releasing the hormone. If the adrenal glands are working normally, cortisol levels should rise.

Shakti's blood work came back with all the classic signs of Addison's, making an initial diagnosis relatively easy: high potassium, low sodium, and high kidney parameters. The emergency veterinarian performed an ACTH test which confirmed the diagnosis.

ACTH test

The only way that your vet can test for Addison's is to perform an ACTH test. At time of writing (August 2009), an ACTH test costs upwards of $200. It's so expensive partly because the veterinarian pays over $70 just for the vial to perform the test.[8]

The ACTH test involves several steps:

- A blood test is taken to determine the baseline cortisol levels.

---

[8] see Novartis Animal Health, 2003

- An injection of ACTH is given.
- An hour or two later, another blood test is taken and cortisol levels are measured.

A normal dog will produce cortisol in response to the ACTH injection. A dog with Addison's will not. The ACTH stimulation test is the gold standard to diagnose Addison's disease—without the test, your dog will not have a confirmed diagnosis. Your practitioner will find low or no cortisol levels before and after administering the ACTH.

Chapter Six: Genetics and Inheritability

According to Dr. Anita Oberbauer—professor at the University of California, Davis Department of Animal Science—dogs are "the most genetically engineered species on the planet" due to a long history of breeding dogs for desirable traits and breeding out undesirable characteristics.

Many years ago, when I was living in the United Kingdom, I bred working Siberian Huskies. I had a basic understanding of genetics—enough to know that when I wanted to breed all-white Siberians into my line, that I had to find a sire and a dam with the recessive and elusive white gene and breed them together. A few months later, my bitch produced a litter of six puppies: three grey and white, two black and white, and one white. This was a result of a little knowledge, and a lot of good luck. Why "luck"? Choosing a sire and dam that carry those traits was nothing more than an educated guess; it isn't possible to tell what genes a dog has just by looking at it. A dog breeder must look at pedigrees and use the laws of probability to breed a trait in, or breed one out.

Not being able to "see" genes are part of the reason why it's difficult to breed out Addison's disease from an affected population like Bearded Collies or Standard Poodles. You can't tell what dogs are carriers for the disease by looking at them, and there's no DNA test (at time of writing) that will tell you which dogs are carriers. However, a basic understanding of genetics and probabilities could prevent a lot of heartache in the future. At a minimum, sires and dams who have produced litters of Addison's pups should not be bred from again unless the breeder is certain which parent has the gene for the disease.

A Standard Poodle breeder friend of mine, "Maggie" bred two of her dogs together and produced six beautiful, healthy puppies. Because the puppies were so perfect, she decided to go for another litter with the same sire and dam a year later. Just before the second litter was born, the first phone call came in from one of the owners of a bitch from the first litter with the bad news: her puppy had just been diagnosed with Addison's disease. Within the next few weeks, three out of six puppies came down with the disease. Maggie was distraught, but informed all of the new owners of the likelihood of Addison's in their new puppies. Within two years, four out of the litter of six puppies came down with Addison's disease.

How inheritability works

Every cell in the body contains DNA, or deoxyribonucleic acid. DNA is made up of repeating pieces of information located on nucleotide bases. The sections of DNA that give instructions on how to make and operate a living organism are called *genes*. The genes are located in compacted sections of DNA called *chromosomes*. Dogs have over 20,000 genes and 38 pairs of chromosomes in each cell (Oberbauer & Bell, n.d.).

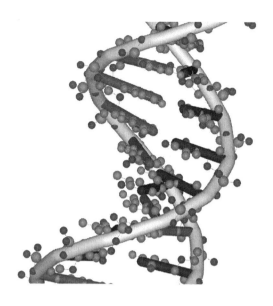

Double helix DNA structure. One section of DNA, like the one depicted here, can be thought of as a gene.

Each pair of non-sex chromosomes is called an *autosome*. Because autosomes come in pairs, each gene has two possible states, called *alleles*. Alleles can be identical (homozygous) or different (heterozygous).

The chromosome(s) responsible for diseases are always found at the same location —for example in Portuguese water dogs, the loci associated with late onset Addison's disease is always chromosomes CFA12 and 37. [9]

---

[9] See Chase et. al, 2006

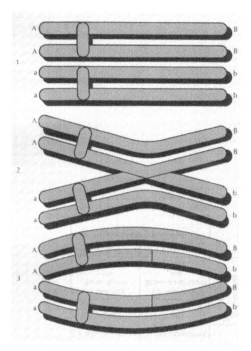

A model of chromosomes.

When a hereditary trait is referred to as *dominant*, it means that if an allele has a certain characteristic (i.e. short legs), it will show up no matter what the other paired allele is coded for. According to Adam Miklósi, author of the book Dog Behavior, evolution and cognition, short legs in dogs is actually a genetic abnormality called achondroplasia, where the legs stop growing during puppyhood. Because short legs are a dominant trait (like brown eyes in humans), a long-legged dog and a short-legged dog can be bred together to result in a short-legged dog every time. By mating dogs together in this way, the abnormality becomes "fixed" in certain dog populations. This resulted in the dachshunds and Chihuahuas of today.

On the other hand, a *recessive* trait means that in order for the trait to appear, two alleles must be exactly the same. An example of a recessive trait is blue eyes in Siberian huskies—in order for the trait to show through, two alleles must carry the gene for blue eye color.

A third type of trait is also possible, called incomplete dominance, where the trait may or may not show through. For example, spots on a dog's coat are an example of incomplete dominance. A dog many have heavy spotting, no spotting, or if they are a heterozygous individual (i.e. one allele is dominant and the other is recessive), they might have mild spotting.

The heritability of a trait is designated with a number from 0 to 1. The designation '0' means that there is no probability of inheriting the trait for a population and that the trait is entirely environmental. Spoken language in humans is an example of a trait that is environmental (heritability=0) as is a cropped tail in dogs (tail docking is performed by people—it is not inherited).[10] A designation of 1 means that there is 100% certainty the trait will show up if the affected allele is present in a population. Blood type is an example of a trait that is inherited

---

[10] Dogs' tail docking has actually been banned in the UK since 2007 by the Animal Welfare Act.

(heritability=1). Dr. Anita Oberbauer (2006) reports that for Portuguese Water Dogs, Addison's disease has an inheritability of 0.49 (+/- 0.16). Dr. Oberbauer's research also suggests that Addison's is most likely due to a recessive mode of inheritance (i.e. two identical alleles are needed for the disease to manifest) and the more inbred an animal is, the higher the likelihood of Addison's; highly inbred dogs in the study had up to a 25% chance of being affected with Addison's disease. Research is continuing in many breeds under CGAP as Dr. Oberbauer's team continues to work on discovering the location of the affected genes on the chromosomes.

However, considering that Addison's disease is 100 times more prevalent in the genetically engineered dog population than in the more diverse human population, it stands to reason that there are genes responsible for Addison's disease and eventually those genes will be identified, enabling dog breeder's to take steps to eradicate the inheritability of the disease in dogs.

Chapter Seven: Treatment Options

A dog in an Addisonian crisis needs specialized care by a veterinarian who will look at several factors before treating your pet. If your pet arrives at the vets with cardiovascular collapse and atrial standstill (a type of heart arrhythmia), aggressive therapy will be needed to correct low blood volume (hypovolemia), electrolyte disturbances (hyponatremia), low levels of cortisol, and a variety of other life-threatening conditions that may be present. Depending on the condition your pet is in at the time, treatment may include the following therapies:[11]

---

[11] Recommended by veterinarians L. Tilley and J. Goodwin, authors of the Manual of Canine and Feline Cardiology

1. IV saline solution to help replace lost electrolytes and other minerals. IV saline can also dilute the high levels of potassium in the blood

2. IV prednisolone sodium succinate or dexamethasone sodium phosphate to replace glucocorticoids

3. Percorten-V or Florinef to replace missing mineralcorticoids

4. IV calcium gluconate to treat life-threatening heart arrythmias

Treatment for Addison's disease in dogs consist of two stages.

Step one is emergency treatment. If your dog is in Addisonian crisis, your vet will want to, at a minimum, start your pet in IV fluids to get the electrolyte levels back to normal. Shakti's crisis emerged within hours of initially getting sick: her legs wobbled, she couldn't walk more than a few feet, she was severely lethargic, barely responding to her name. Her heart rate was slow and the rhythm was off. The IV fluids administered at the emergency veterinarians temporarily restored electrolyte imbalances and saved her life.

The second step of treatment is maintenance therapy, which involves supplementing the missing hormones for the rest of your pet's life. There is no one universal "fix" for Addison's disease: dogs will need to be closely monitored to reach optimal health levels. Treatment will also depend on whether your dog has primary or secondary Addison's disease.

Treatment for Primary Addison's Disease

Your pet will need lifelong cortisol and aldosterone replacements. You have two options: either Florinef (fludrocortisone) or DOCP (Percorten-V) and prednisone. *Despite claims from manufacturers, herbs and natural remedies cannot replace missing hormones.*

Fludrocortisone–marketed under the brand name Florinef, replaces both cortisol (a glucocorticoid) and aldosterone (a mineralocorticoid). The single medication may be all that your dog needs. Dosage recommendations are 0.02 mg/kg/day (approximately one pill per ten pounds of body weight). A drawback with fludrocortisone is that it is very expensive– treatment can cost hundreds of dollars a month for a large dog.[12]

Percorten-V replaces aldosterone and is administered once a month. In addition to the monthly shot, dogs on Percorten-V will need to take daily doses of prednisone to replace cortisol. The cost varies wildly depending on where you obtain your Percorten-V from. For our 40lb border collie, local veterinarians charge from $50-78 for one 1.33 ml dose (1 1/3

---

[12] You can find an online calculator for Florinef and Percorten-V at www.addisonsindogs.com.

vials) of Percorten-V and 30 5mg tablets of prednisone, including the office visit.

Side effects of medication

Medications for Addison's disease have many possible side effects. If your dog is experiencing any problems, it may because they are receiving too much medication: speak with your veterinarian about lowering the dose.

Percorten-V side effects:

- Hypernatremia (high levels of salt in the blood)
- Hypokalemia (low blood potassium)
- Polyuria (excessive urination)
- Polydipsia (excessive thirst)
- Increased blood volume
- Edema (fluid retention)—watch for excessive weight gain
- Weight loss
- Cardiac enlargement
- Depression
- Anorexia (i.e. not eating)

- Skin and coat changes
- Diarrhea
- Vomiting
- Weakness
- Incontinence
- Pain on injection
- Injection site abscess

Prednisone Side Effects and Florinef (fludrocortisone acetate) Side Effects

Prednisone and Florinef have similar side effects because Florinef has glucocorticoid properties and acts like prednisone. These include:

- Hunger
- Loss of hair
- Muscle atrophy (wasting)
- Panting
- Urinating and drinking excessively
- Poor quality coat

- Frequent skin infections

- Thinning skin

- Vomiting

- Diarrhea

- Other gastrointestinal upsets

- Excessive weight gain

- Diabetes mellitus

- Elevated liver enzymes

- Lipidemia (excess fat in the blood)

Unfortunately, the side effects of these drugs can mimic other disorders that are common in Addison's disease (i.e. hypothyroidism) and even Addison's disease itself, so it's vitally important to have your pet's blood checked for electrolyte imbalances and other disorders. You should speak with your veterinarian before reducing any medications.

Treatment for Secondary Addison's Disease

An atypical Addisonian dog with normal electrolyte levels only requires glucocorticoids replacement, i.e. prednisone, hydrocortisone, dexamethasone or similar replacement. Veterinarians used to recommend that owners salt their pet's food, but it appears that has fallen out of practice and is no longer thought to be necessary. Generic glucocorticoid replacements are typically cheap and run only a few dollars per month.

Dosages for all medications are approximate: your pet may vary in the amount of medication it needs and your veterinarian may want to tinker with the dosage, monitoring electrolytes and other functions until your dog's health is at an optimal level.

What happens if my dog doesn't receive prednisone?

Prednisone replaces cortisol and has a glucocorticoid effect. Unlike mineralcorticoids, a lack of glucocorticoids isn't likely to cause an immediate, life-threatening situation. However, a lack of glucocorticoids means that your dog will not be able to physically deal with stress; this can lead to an Addisonian crisis.

According to Dr. R. Bowen at Colorado State University, glucocorticoid activity in a dog's body comes from cortisol (also called hydrocortisone). Every cell in the body has cortisol, and every system is affected by a lack of cortisol. However, the most notable problems with a lack of cortisol include aiding the body maintain proper glucose levels and maintaining the immune system.

Cortisol is released when adrenocorticotropic hormone (ACTH) is secreted from the pituitary gland. ACTH works when your pet is under stress–this could be as simple as leaving them alone in the house, a thunderstorm, or raising your voice. The lack of glucocorticoids will interfere with the complex regulatory systems that deals with stress; without glucocorticoids, an Addison's dog will go into overload and will suffer from an Addisonian crisis.

Chapter Eight: Cheaper Treatment Options

If your dog has canine Addison's disease, you might experience sticker shock at the veterinary office. A month's supply of replacement hormones could cost over two hundred dollars a month for a large dog. However, it is possible to reduce the cost of treatment, or even get it for free!

1. Shop Around for Percorten-V and Florinef

At diagnosis, our border collie, Shakti, weighed 33 lbs. One shot of Percorten-V (1.33ml) cost $69 at the veterinarian. On top of that, we had to pay $15 for prednisone every 20 days. I did a little shopping around and reduced our monthly cost from $80 to $55 for all medicines.

2. Google is your friend, but don't expect miracles: the cheapest price for a 4ml bottle of Percorten-V I found on the internet at time of writing was $150 ("on sale"). I followed one ad for $138.50 to a generic pet .com website but when I got there–surprise, surprise the price had jumped to $179.99. Even if I could get a vial of Percorten-V at $138.50, that's still $46.16 per dose…and you have to buy the needles and administer it yourself on top of that.

3. Try compounding pharmacies (pharmacies that provide individualized prescription drugs as opposed to commercially prepared drugs) for cheap Florinef (also ask about liquid Florinef, which is another option). Here are a few to consider:

   Nora Apothecary (http://www.noraapothecary.com)

   1 (800) 729-0276

   Congaree Veterinary Pharmacy (http://www.congareevetrx.com)

   1 (877) 939-1335

   Valley Drug and Compounding (http://www.1pharmacy.com)

   1 (818) 788-0635

   Pet Pharm (http://www.petpharm.org)

Summit Chemist (http://www.svprx.ca) (in Canada)
1-866-794-7387

4. Find the cheapest vet around and give him your business: There's a well-known pet clinic in my city called Herschel Animal Clinic. They don't have the bells and whistles of the upscale veterinary practices (they rarely answer their phone and there's no brightly lit, cushy waiting room—sometimes you have to wait out in the parking lot for an hour or two to be seen). But they are cheap, and for someone with an Addisonian dog, that can literally be a lifesaver. We're charged only $45 per 1.33ml shot of Percorten-V, and a month's supply of prednisone is $10. Shakti and I take a book, a bone, and a Starbucks, and just enjoy the time together while we wait.

5. Cut down on the dosage of Percorten-V/Florinef with your vet's help: since being diagnosed with Addison's, Shakti has put on ten pounds (she looks healthier now). However, her medication (1.33ml) has stayed the same. Technically, the dosage should have been increased but as her blood work is fine, there's no need. Tell your vet that you would like to decrease your pet's medication. Your vet will check your pet's electrolytes every month for a few months until you've reached the lowest maintenance

dose possible. Initially, this will be expensive, say $50 per month for the additional blood work for 6 months. But it might save you $20-30 a month thereafter in decreased Percorten-V or Florinef.

Finally, if you can't afford it, find a way to afford it: one reason that Dr. Plant at Herschel offers Percorten-V at the lowest price possible is because he knows it's sometimes prohibitively expensive. One former client of his just didn't get the treatment for their dog, and the animal "just wasted away," he said. "It was sad, sad." The fact is, your dog must have replacement hormones, or they will die. Although there isn't a free pet clinic system in the states like there is in the UK (the PSDA), there are many routes you can try to obtain reduced cost, or even free, care.

- Write a letter to your vet: this will probably work if you've been a long term client and are likely to continue being a client in the future. Write a personal letter and tell him that you cannot afford full treatment costs. Tell him what you *can* afford a month. Ask him/her for their help. Remember that your vet will still have to purchase the drug at base cost ($45 for a 1.33ml dose!), so don't expect miracles. But it's worth a shot (if you'll excuse the pun).

- Contact shelters and rescue organizations in your area and ask them if they know of any low cost clinics. One website—www.pets911.com, offers a search feature where you can enter your zip code and find local rescue and animal organizations that may be able to help.

- Consider finding another home for your pet. If you have a purebred animal, contact your nearest breed-specific rescue and tell them that you are having trouble affording medications. Some rescue organizations will allow you to advertise for a new home on their website, and someone who is familiar with Addison's might be willing to give your dog a home. You can also look for breed-specific rescue discussion boards—there are many on the web. Whatever you do, make sure that you don't give your animal to the local animal control or city-run shelter; they immediately euthanize sick animals.

- Make A Wish: if all else fails you can try posting for help on the Make a Wish page at http://www.wishuponahero.com. They match donors to people with needs. You never know when an angel (maybe a local vet?) will offer a helping hand!

Long Term Stress Management

Because your dog cannot produce stress hormones, they'll need extra prednisone whenever they are more likely to be stressed. Our vet advised us to give Shakti one extra pill:

- Whenever she gets sick
- If she needs hospitalization
- In case of trauma

It's especially important for dogs with Addison's disease to receive fluids if they have to undergo general anesthesia.

Owning a dog with Addison's disease can seem overwhelming at first—both emotionally and financially. However, dogs with Addison's disease—properly treated—live just as long as their disease-free counterparts.

Appendix 1

A note on heartworm preventative medicines.

Do you give your Addison's dog Heartguard or Advantage for heartworm control? These medicines can put a major stress load on your dog and come with a whole host of potential side effects.

Product information found inside the Advantage package states that you should not give the medication to breeding, pregnant or lactating dogs, small dogs or puppies under seven weeks old. Merial states that Heartguard is safe for puppies over six weeks. However, neither medication has been safety tested on Addison's dogs, and the list of possible side effects is disturbing:

Merial lists the side effects from Heartguard as anorexia, ataxia (lack of coordination of muscle movements), convulsions, depression/lethargy, diarrhea, hypersalivation (excess drooling), mydriasis (pupil dilation), staggering, and vomiting, 1 out of 100 dogs will experience vomiting and/or diarrhea. In clinical trials, Advantage didn't fare much better: Bayer reported that 10% of dogs had itching and scratching, 1.5 percent of dogs stopped eating and the same percentage became lethargic. Other side effects reported including a dog becoming depressed and weak several days after application of the medicine, bloody stools, coughing, lethargy and eye/nose discharge. Granted, these side effects usually occur at higher doses and not with the low doses found for heartworm treatement—but considering your Addison's dog is immune compromised, you may want to consider alternatives.

Heartguard also comes with a strong warning for Collie owners; collies and related breeds (i.e. Shetland sheepdogs, Australian shepherds, or Old English sheepdogs) may be more sensitive to the Heartguard ingredients. Out of five Ivermectin-Sensitive collies who were tested in clinical trials, four had to be euthanized after receiving Heartguard. There is a test that your veterinarian can perform to detect ivermectin sensitivity: a DNA test for P-glycoprotein mutation identifies ivermectin sensitive dogs.

Obviously, your decision to give Heartguard or Advantage to your dog will depend upon many factors, including where you live, what condition your Addison's dog is in, and what risk factors your dog has for mosquito bites. You'll want to discuss these risk factors with your veterinarian so that you can decide whether it's worth giving these medicines to your Addison's dog.

Appendix 2: Web Resources

Addison's in dogs website, where you can find Florinef and Percorten-V dosage calculators and more information on canine Addison's disease:

http://www.addisonsindogs.com/

Intervet: Alternative vaccine manufacturer

http://www.intervetusa.com/

Heska: Alternative vaccine manufacturer

http://www.heska.com/careers/careers.asp

Make A Wish: a website where you can ask donors for help:

http://www.wishuponahero.com.

Pets 911 site: search for rescue and animal organizations:

http://www.pets911.com

Canine Genetic Analysis Project (CGAP). A research program working on identifying the genetic markers in certain dog breeds:

http://cgap.ucdavis.edu/

Definitions

Adrenocorticotropic hormone (ACTH) stimulation test: This test signals the adrenal glands to produce cortisol. If the adrenal glands are working normally, cortisol levels should rise.

Addisonian crisis: a medical emergency involving several factors including shock, cardiovascular collapse, atrial standstill, low blood volume and electrolyte disturbances.

Adrenal cortex: part of the adrenal glands that secrete glucocorticoids like cortisol and mineralocorticoids like aldosterone.

Adrenal Glands: Part of the body responsible for regulation of stress hormones that lies behind the kidneys. Consists of two parts: inner medulla and outer cortex. The adrenal cortex secretes glucocorticoids like cortisol and mineralocorticoids like aldosterone.

Aldosterone: a corticosteroid hormone secreted by the adrenal cortex which regulates salt and water balance in the body

Atrial standstill: a heart arrhythmia caused by electrolyte imbalances, particularly high potassium levels. Can be reversed in Addison's by rapid infusion of IV fluids.

Atypical Addison's disease: where only the cortisol producing part of the adrenal cortex isn't working *or* Addison's dogs who present without the classic electrolyte changes (i.e. low sodium and high potassium) seen in primary Addison's.

Azotemia: elevated kidney parameters, i.e. high urea in the blood as shown by the serum BUN (blood urea nitrogen) level test.

Bradycardia: slow heart rate.

BUN (blood urea nitrogen) level test: used to detect elevated kidney parameters.

Calcium gluconate: a mineral supplement usually used to correct low levels of calcium in the blood (hypocalcemia) and heart arrhythmias.

Capillary Refill Time: the time is takes for blood to refill empty capillaries. Normal capillary refill time in a healthy dog is 1 second.

Cortisol: a glucocorticoid hormone secreted by the adrenal cortex that regulates blood sugar.

Cardiovascular collapse: sudden failure of the heart to pump blood.

Corticosteroid: a class of hormones produced by the adrenal glands that includes glucocorticoids and mineralcorticoids.

Cortisol: a stress-fighting glucocorticoid produced by the adrenal gland.

Edema: swelling causes by excessive accumulation of water in the body.

Electrolytes: salts found in the blood such as sodium, potassium and calcium.

Florinef: a brand name glucocorticoid and mineralcorticoid replacement.

Glucocorticoid: hormones produced by the adrenal glands that affect multiple body systems including appetite stimulation, maintaining blood glucose levels and controlling water, calcium, and red/white blood cell levels in the blood.

Hematemesis: vomiting blood.

Hyperkalemia: elevated potassium level due to lack of the adrenal hormone aldosterone.

Hypernatremia: high levels of salt in the blood (an electrolyte imbalance).

Hypochloremia: an electrolyte disturbance characterized by low levels of chloride ions in the blood.

Hypocholesterolemia: low levels of cholesterol in the blood.

Hypocortisolism: low levels of cortisol in the blood.

Hypokalemia: low levels of potassium in the blood.

Hyponatremia: low levels of salt in the blood.

Hypoproteinemia: low level of protein in the blood.

Hypothyroidism: underproduction of hormones by the thyroid gland. Can lead to weight gain, dry skin, and constipation.

Hypovolemia: a decreased amount of blood circulating in the body.

Ketoconazole: a medication used to treat fungal infections.

Melena: dark, tarry stools (usually a product of blood in the stool).

Metabolic acidosis: overly acidic blood.

Mineralocorticoid: hormones secreted by the adrenal cortex that regulate salt and water balance in the body. Mineralcorticoid deficiency leads to high potassium levels, low salt levels, and poor heart function. Aldosterone has major mineralcorticoid activity in the body but cortisol also plays a minor part.

Percorten-V: a medication that replaces mineralcorticoids in the body.

Phagocytes: white blood cells (immune cells) that digest invading particles.

Pituitary gland: the gland at the base of the brain that is responsible for cortisol production. The pituitary gland produces adrenocorticotropic hormone (ACTH) which signals the adrenal glands to produce cortisol.

Polydipsia: excessive thirst.

Polyuria: excessive urination.

Potassium: a mineral that is essential for body function (an electrolyte).

Prednisolone: prednisone's active metabolite.

Prednisone: a corticosteroid replacement (otherwise referred to as cortisol replacement or stress hormone replacement). Usually given in combination with Percorten-V in primary Addison's or as a stand-alone drug in secondary Addison's.

Primary Addison's disease: the classic Addison's disease where the adrenal glands stop producing both mineralcorticoids and glucocorticoids.

Stress Leukogram: a characteristic white blood cell pattern that sick dogs normally exhibit as a result of cortisol release. Because Addison's dogs do not release cortisol, the absence of a stress leukogram in a blood panel is a hallmark for the disease.

Trichuriasis: whipworm. Causes similar symptoms to Addison's disease.

Typical Addison's disease: adrenal glands that are not producing both cortisol and aldosterone.

References

American Animal Hospital Association. Report of the American Animal Hospital Association (AAHA) Canine Vaccine Task Force: 2003 Canine Vaccine Guidelines, Recommendations, and Supporting Literature. 2003. Article posted on website *Journal of the American Animal Hospital Association.* Retrieved July 21, 2009 from: http://www.jaaha.org/cgi/content/citation/42/2/80/T1

Bayer healthcare: Animal care division. Advantage Multi for Dogs product information. Article posted on Bayer healthcare: Animal care division. Retrieved August 13, 2009 from: http://www.bayerdvm.com/Resources/Docs/Advantage-Multi-Dog-Label.pdf

Bowen R.. Glucocorticoids. Article posted on website *Colorado State University.* Retrieved August 1, 2009 from: http://www.vivo.colostate.edu/hbooks/pathphys/endocrine/adrenal/gluco.html may 26, 2006.

Case, L. *The Dog: Its Behavior, Nutrition and Health.* 2nd ed. Hoboken, NJ: Wiley-Blackwell. 2005.

Chase K, Sargan D, Miller K, Ostrander E, Lark K. Understanding the genetics of autoimmune disease: two loci that regulate late onset Addison's disease in Portuguese Water Dogs. Int J Immunogenet. 2006 Jun;33(3):179-84.

Coyne M., Burr J, Yule T, Harding M, Tresnan D, McGavin D, Duration of immunity in dogs after vaccination or naturally acquired infection. 2001. *The Veterinary Record.* 149: 509-515.A

Davidson G, and. Plumb D. Ketoconazole. *Veterinary drug handbook-client edition.* Article posted on website Aboretum View Animal Hospital. Retrieved aug 13, 2009 from http://avah.org/pdf/systemic/Ketoconazole.pdf

Duval, D. & Giger, U. Vaccine associated immune-mediated hemolytic anaemia in the dog. *Journal of Veterinary Internal Medicine.* 10, 290-295.

Forney B. Prednisone for veterinary use. Article posted on website *Wedgewood Pharmacy.* Retrieved August 1, 2009 from: http://www.wedgewoodpharmacy.com

Hughes A, Nelson R, Famula T, Bannasch D. Clinical features and heritability of hypoadrenocorticism in Nova Scotia Duck Tolling Retrievers: 25 cases (1994–2006) *JAVMA*, Vol 231, No. 3, August 1, 2007

Kaufman J. Diseases of the adrenal cortex of dogs and cats. *Mod Vet Pract* 1984;65:513–516.

Kintzer PP, Peterson ME. Diagnosis and management of primary spontaneous hypoadrenocorticism (Addison's disease) in dogs. *Semin Vet Med Surg (Small Anim)* 1994;9:148–152.

Klingborg DJ, Hustead DR, Curry-Galvin EA, et al. AVMA Council on Biologic and Therapeutic Agents' report on cat and dog vaccines. J Am Vet Med Assoc 2002;221:1401–1407.

Klingborg DJ, Hustead DR, Curry-Galvin EA, et al. AVMA Council on Biologic and Therapeutic Agents' report on cat and dog vaccines. J Am Vet Med Assoc 2002;221:1401–1407.

Little C, Marshall C, Downs J. Addison's disease in the dog. Vet Rec 1989;124:469–470.

McCaskill B. Addison's Disease--a better understanding for Westie owners. 2003. Article posted on website Westie foundation of Americ, Inc. Retrieved August 12, 2009 from: http://www.westiefoundation.org/newsletter/03addisons.htm

McCaw DL, Thompson M, Tate D, Bonderer A Chen Y. Serum distemper virus and parvovirus antibody titers among dogs brought to a veterinary hospital for revaccination. Journal of the American Veterinary Medical Association. J Am Vet Med Assoc. 1998 Jul 1;213(1):72-5.

Merial. Heartguard Chewables Product Information. Article posted on website Merial.com. Retrieved august 10, 2009 from: http://heartgard.us.merial.com/downloads/Dog_information.pdf

Moore,G, Glickman, L. A perspective on vaccine guidelines and titer tests for dogs, *Journal of the American Veterinary Medical*

Association, January 15, 2004, Vol. 224, No. 2, Pages 200-203

Novartis Animal Health. *Addison's Disease: Uncommon or Underdiagnosed?* Thomson Veterinary Healthcare Communications, Lenexa, Kan, 2003.

Novartis Animal Health. Heartguard, Protection to live. Article posted on website Merial.com. Retrieved August 9, 2009 from: http://heartgard.us.merial.com/home/

Oberbauer A. Genetic evaluation of Addison's disease in the Portuguese Water Dog. *BMC Vet Res* - 01-JAN-2006; 2: 15

Oberbauer A. & Bell D, Genetics Primer. Article posted on website *Tualatin Kennel Club*. Retrieved August 19, 2009 from: http://www.tualatinkc.org/pdf/Genetics%20Primer.pdf

Oberbauer A, Benemann K, Belanger J, Wagner D, Ward J, Famula T, Inheritance of hypoadrenocorticism in Bearded Collies *AJVR,* Vol 63, No. 5, May 2002

Olson P, Klingeborn B, Hedhammar A. Serum antibody response to canine parvovirus, canine adenovirus-1, and canine distemper virus in dogs with known status of immunization: study of dogs in Sweden. *Am J Vet Res* 1988;49:1460–1466.

OSU Boren Veterinary Medical Teaching Hospital. *Oklahoma State University College for Veterinary Sciences.* Retrieved July 20, 2009 from http://www. http://www.cvhs.okstate.edu

Paul MA, Appel M, Barrett R, et al. Report of the American Animal Hospital Association (AAHA) Canine Vaccine Task Force: executive summary and 2003 canine vaccine guidelines and recommendations. *J Am Anim Hosp Assoc* 2003;39:119–131

Plotnick A, Addison's Disease: Averting An Adrenal Crisis. *Dog World* 86 (6), June 2001, p. 54.

Richards M Corticosteriod side effects. Article posted on website Vet Info. Retrieved august 9, 2009 from: http://www.vetinfo.com/ceffect.html

The Bearded Collie Foundation for Health. Addison's Disease (Hypoadrenocorticism). Article posted on website *Beacon for Health*. Retrieved July 20, 2009. http://www.beaconforhealth.org/addisons_main.html

Tilley L, Goodwin J. Manual of Canine and Feline Cardiology. Philadelphia, Pennsylvania: Saunders. 3 edition (January 15, 2001)

Twark L, Dodds WJ. Clinical use of serum parvovirus and distemper virus antibody titers for determining revaccination strategies in healthy dogs. J Am Vet Med Assoc 2000;217:1021–1024.

Acknowledgments

Rendering of DNA picture by Ghutchis @ Flickr.com

Chromosomes by A Journey Around My Skull @ Flickr.com

Index

ACTH, 11, 12, 14, 16, 35, 36, 52, 63, 67

Addisonian crisis, 19, 21, 45, 51, 52, 63

adrenal cortex, 14, 15, 16, 34, 63, 64, 66, 70

adrenal glands, 11, 13, 14, 15, 23, 24, 35, 63, 67, 68

adrenal insufficiency, 13

adrenocorticotropic hormone, 11, 14, 35, 52, 63, 67

adrenocorticotropic hormone stimulation, 11, 35

aldosterone, 14, 15, 16, 33, 47, 63, 68

American Veterinary Medical Association, 30, 71, 72

atrial standstill, 45, 63

atypical Addison's, 15

azotemia, 33

booster shots, 26, 27

bradycardia, 11, 20

BUN (blood urea nitrogen), 33

calcium gluconate, 46

cancer, 24

Canine Genetic Analysis Project (CGAP), 24

capillary refill time, 20, 64

cardiovascular collapse, 45, 63

compounding pharmacies, 54

cortisol, 13, 15, 34, 35, 36, 45, 47, 52, 63, 66, 68

DNA, 38, 39, 40, 60, 75

Edema, 48

electrolyte changes, 15, 64

electrolytes, 11, 15, 45, 51, 55

Florinef, 46, 47, 49, 53, 54, 55, 61

genes, 38, 39, 43

genetics, 25, 37, 38, 69

glucocorticoid, 47, 49, 51, 52, 64

granulomatous disease, 23

hematemesis, 21

hyperkalemia, 33

Hypernatremia, 48

hypoadrenocorticism, 13

hypochloremia, 33

hypocholesterolemia, 34

hypocortisolism, 13

Hypokalemia, 48

hyponatremia, 33, 45, 63

hypoproteinemia, 34

hypothyroidism, 50

hypovolemia, 45, 63

IV fluids, 8, 11, 20, 46

Ketoconazole, 24

Make A Wish, 57

medication, 12, 47, 48, 51, 55, 59

melena, 21

metabolic acidosis, 34

Percorten-V, 46, 47, 48, 53, 54, 55, 56

Pfizer, 28

phagocytes, 23

pituitary gland, 14, 16, 24, 25, 52

Polydipsia, 48

Polyuria, 48

potassium, 11, 15, 33, 34, 35, 45, 48, 65, 66

prednisolone, 46

prednisone, 47, 49, 51, 53, 55, 58

Primary Addison's, 15

sodium, 11, 15, 33, 34, 35, 46

stress leukogram, 34

stress, controlling, 58

symptoms, 17, 19, 20, 21, 24

titer test, 29, 30, 31

treatment, cheaper options, 53

trichuriasis, 34

Typical Addison's, 15

vaccinations, 23, 25, 26, 30

Sterling had normal Sodium + Potassium levels.
Atypical Addisons is when only a part of the adrenal cortex isn't working.
Primary Addisons Disease
Atypical —

Cost of medication - ?
Percorton -
Prednison - Is the canine meds - 1mg - 5mg - 10mg etc. different from human prednison?